PULLING AT THE CURTAIN

Pulling
At the
Curtain

MARY JANE PHILPY-DOLLINS

ISBN: 979-8-218-46901-6
Library of Congress Control Number: 2024917992

Cover image: Photoongraphy, Shutterstock

Contents

"Praise our choices, sisters, for each doorway
open to us was taken by squads of fighting
women who paid years of trouble and struggle,
who paid their wombs, their sleep, their lives
that we might walk through these gates upright."

—MARGE PIERCY,
"THE SABBATH OF MUTUAL RESPECT"

PULLING AT THE CURTAIN

The Sprint

I
morning commute
sencha green in hand
the sky is not awake

a Range Rover ahead
silver Mercedes behind

on my left, a rabbit
attempts a sprint
too slowly   he rolls
back and ghastly forth

the SUV keeps moving—
I swerve
I can't stop
I will be late to work

II
my destination looms
solid and purposeful—
a birthday every few hours,
beady sweat and trickling
blood, screams
of new mothers
teary and joyful and
alive

during my shift,
I take 12,481 steps
2 water breaks and
3 Spanish-only patients

I can't slow down
to celebrate every lullaby

III
on the way home, my car zips
past this morning's crime scene—

no blood in the street

I turn down the bleating jazz
and the movement of the day
catches in my throat

I didn't have time to stop

Family Planning

Fertility charts. Ovulation testing. Procreative sex. So these are the first rounds of as-God-intended before she *tries more serious medical intervention.*

The furrowed eyebrows threaten. Her feet cringe in the sterile stirrups. Watching her, my feet are cold. The nurses scurry down the hallway: so many patients to impregnate. What a useless nursing student I've turned out to be.

As I tune out the specialist, I ponder our scheduled sex life. *We're trying,* we've said, the haughty optimism of carefree sex equals instant baby. For now, it's still you and me in the honeycomb sheets, sweaty in the magic of making new flesh with fluids and faith.

When she cries into the blue paper gown, I see the future for us: the dirty talk that fails, the grudging invitation to the stiff whitecoats, the clinical threesome of *let's get this done.* I hand her a tissue. I follow the stethoscope into the robin's egg hallway. Is this what I want?

Nightmare

A positive is no longer a negative or is it? I wonder aloud
on the Senate floor as the blood-red Lieutenant Governor
opens his mouth to speak directly to my husband
about my potential. One hand holds a ticking bomb,
the other holds my uterus, my fallopians flopping
on the ancient carpet, trailing behind him as he tap-dances
to the podium. To vote? To vote! with my hands bound
behind me, to live as my puppy dog sees me, upside down
with an upturned chin, both of us darling and unable to speak.
As I wait in the corner, I'm screaming right in the ear
of this windbag jerk who holds my uterus in his hand—
a triumph for his donor base, a trophy for his wall.

Hemorrhage

On my 34th hour of work,
I pad into Room 1891,
a routine safety check.

I smile politely,
ask her about the pain,
mechanically lift the sheet.
A pool of crimson
balloons between her thighs
the same color as the EMERGENCY
button I punch,
and I wait
fif-
teen
et-
er-
nal
seconds for help.
In broken Spanish, I
stumble to explain why.

Another nurse bursts into the room,
grinds hands of steel
into this stranger's belly.
Two,
three,
four
blood clots emerge,
wild and fecund and warm—
the scarlet trickle
persists. I attach
the IV saltwater, I cling
to the blood pressure

cuff. I clutch
the phone, wait
for direction.

Give her the shot, the doctor sighs—
I'm too busy to help you now.
I locate the muscle, jab
the needle, wait
for the blood to stop.

As we massage her uterus,
the patient giggles. I've never seen
someone so unmoved by danger.

I hang the bag,
chart her stats,
take
a
breath.

Her young daughters crowd the bed.
They turn to me,
a trickle of questions building to a flood.
 What's a uterus?
 Why's there so much blood?
 Will she be okay?

I don't know what they know
and I'm not sure they want to know

that today we saved her life.

Try to Keep Up

how quickly it is 5am already behind running running to keep up
with the demands of other people's needs real and imagined the space
between *what can I do for you* and *what more do you need from me*
makes me claustrophobic—do I have time for a teachable moment?
sterile water and red dye simulate a hemorrhage—a mannequin and
a new graduate nurse work together to practice how to save the baby
save her life save the sanity that is left after I watched my patient bleed
and bleed and bleed on my last shift and this place doesn't have time
for your scaredy-cat questions so get in there and push the meds STAT
versus urgent versus routine and *will you write the order please*—how I
hope my words are paced enough for your husband to follow in English
Español Medicalese and all I want is a break to eat the sad lunch I
packed 17 hours ago but can't because you call me with needs every
time the sandwich hits my lips will I take you to the bathroom will I
bring you green jello when can you have more pain meds—and *can you
call for report?*

I practice the brisk
parade—the revolving door
never satisfied

Doubt

I start the day with a pregnancy test
and end the day with blood.

I can't decide if this period is an end
or a chance to restart.

What mother I've been to daydreams—
what staggering doubt a tampon brings.

Am I too old to try?

How long should we labor
in delusions? How this fantasy aches.

The bloody underwear
mocks me from the laundry—

how ready I was to fill
the old basket with tiny striped socks,
onesies straight out of the plastic.

Escape Plan

Today the mercury will be
a hundred and eleven.

I walk home from
the glitz and brass—
last night's miniskirt,
my hair flouffed
into a bun of no regrets.
I couldn't find my shoes.

The metallic *ping-ping*
of the slot machines assaults me,
a too-bright cringe in the chilly room.
We have a winner!
A geriatric bag-of-bones
in a fanny pack plays the penny slots
as a high-haired cocktail
waitress picks at her hem.
The cherry bowl is almost empty.

Upstairs,
my keycard clicks
and the eager sun elbows in—
an unwanted guest in the gaudy king-size.
I drop like a rhinestone
right into the 500-count.

I praise the moving blackout.

The Point

Side by side, we sit on Monday's
saddest couch. The Samsung sells us
on titanic humans, pushing and
shoving and lumbering in
every direction at once, chasing imaginary
numbers. You yell at the referee and nothing
changes. My hands dance with metal points
as the acrylic soft winds through
my muscle memory—a knit there, a yarn
-over here, a quiet celebration of lace.
I don't yell at anyone. An aging favorite
narrates the rising swell—a win in the making.
My fingers build ghosts on the walls of this room
and I know that there is nothing
more real than the light and the shadow and me.

A Lot to Unpack

After Saturday night in a foreign city,
I toss the American Tourister
on the right side of the bed,
pull out
the laundry, re-settle
the jewelry. I can't help
fingering the lacy
lilac thong I never
wore to impress you.
The matching bra
tangles in the cotton pile.
In the cheap seats,
we saw a comedy show, listened
to the Funnyman joke about the art of pussy-licking—
the grooves of an unknown woman,
the hearty guffaws,
an audience full of hipsters.
I heard your laughter, caught
my throat, kept
my tongue to myself.

How to Knit Yourself Together

This project is a long-term tutorial about how to ensure that your life is equally interesting, confusing, contradictory, and unclear. This project knits one full-size adult woman. (Psychological sustainability not guaranteed.)

Materials:
- A childhood in polite society (preferably in a rural area with old money)
- Early religious training (the more sheltered, the better)
- 42" bust, 37" waist, and 50" hips
- A long-standing and unhealthy relationship to your body

Note: *Neutral colors used here look like moral fiber, but will create a less interesting adult woman. Consider using a variegated personality to bring out the pattern.*

Pattern:
Cast on the 1982 Book of Common Prayer with 3 generations of circular logic. Join and place birthday marker. Do not twist your panties.

Row 1: Follow the rules.
Row 2: Follow your bliss.

Repeat Rows 1 & 2 for 41 years.

For additional interest, consider adding these enhancements intermittently without clear external direction:
- Bobbles of uncertainty = seeds of doubt, rebellion, or self-awareness (worked over a weekend yoga retreat or a sexy text message)
- Purls of wisdom = dad jokes, tattoos, formal educational training (worked over 2–4 years with no free time)

- Non-reversible cables and mergers = marriage, business partnerships, unexpected six-degrees-of-Kevin-Bacon (worked in a maybe/maybe not pattern)

Note: Missed stitches should be considered against the wider fabric— use discretion about fixing them on future rows. Some mistakes may be unfixable or may further enhance the design.

Bind off when you are tired of the bullshit, are feeling most alive or when the body is finished with this world. Cut ties and weave in anything left unsaid.

Dark Rooms

When I think of the Ford Festiva,
I think of the morning drive to fifth grade—stalled
en route for you to vomit at the curb,
your migraine fighting back.

I have migraines now, too—
$21 for a little white capsule,
a solution for the family legacy
of dark rooms and unceasing pressure.

When I think about dark rooms,
the frigid quiet of our brick house yanks
me back—how small I tried to make
myself, a daily effort to not be heard.

Even now I know you don't
see me.

Instead, I'll try to see you—
the adult, the complicated, the unknowable—
the woman who showed me
how to make chocolate chip cookies,
the one who fell in love with Rod Stewart,
the one who taught me to sing.

Theology 101

On Sunday, I spend
my morning hours
hoping for revelation,
but all I get is an ache
from the kneelers.

Communion doesn't help.

I want to believe
in Divinity,
but I can't seem to lift the book
of hymns and psalms. My eyes
glaze over the Gospels.

...

On Wednesday, I see the Source
in the emerald grass—
the joy lush
between my toes,
blades full of songs.

Throaty cicadas hum
an afternoon prayer.

Great whites drift
lazy in the blazing
sky—I see a drooling
baby, a chariot
of marshmallows.

...

I inhale the incense
and the open air, touch

the live oaks
and the elder pews.

I let the shadows drip
from my fingers.

Six Months In

Today
love is

a cup of tea
on a Sunday morning

your feet curled with mine

as we read about the world

Invitation

step right up for a closer look—
the staccato rhythm of life
through our bedroom window
    I'm here
    he's not
    we are
    open
    closed

I undress alone in the afternoon
through the open window—
    watch me
    or don't

unashamed, I stare across—
their kitchen shining
their new glass door
    mac & cheese for the toddler
    Merlot for the adults
what fantasy a window makes

from here, I'm shielded from
    the baby's endless shrieks
    the housewife's tragic Jazzercise
    the tension of will-they-work-it-out

I'm sure
they don't watch me at all

July 4th

we sit at the end
of the dock waiting
for the sky to explode

expectant parents set
up checkered blankets
kids chase terriers on polished lawns
sunscreen floats in the air
Yankee Doodle runs his mouth

you lay your hand
on my stale thigh
I sigh in your cheap cologne

after the flash-bang
all that's left
is gray smoke shadows

how soon they disappear

Influence

How cool I tried to be at thirteen:
  that bold fluorescent scrunchie
  a proud hand to my hip
  a silver cross on my neck

What I would say to her now:

vampires are not real
churchgoing gossip is

your hips are
not only for birthing

someday, you will see yourself
beyond what the Polaroid remembers

How to Sink or Swim

when the time comes

you will know
where to sit up straight
when to wear pearls
how not to be an embarrassment
to the Blue Hairs on the third row
    they are always watching
    will tattle to your vain grandmother
    will never ask you a real question

you will know
where to place the salad fork
when to use your inside voice
how to bury your anger

you will know
where to find the floral bathroom
in that frozen house
where one mirror faces another
to make an instant infinity of you—
    a whirligig beetle in a still pond

morning prayer

sugar, spice and everything nice,
my inner voice whispers over and over
heavy organ pedals press
lecherous thoughts
gentle but firm
sacrilegious notes
my fingers press
right there
there
secret skin
wicked
ecstasy
emphatic, desperate
there!
delirious music
in my hidden folds
    what holy joy
my choir sings
and the tall brass tubes explode—
Alleluia, Alleluia

Middle Age

I used to see the tops
of the trees as horizons
for fantasy treehouses
an endless summer of impossible
climbing, buoyant
bare feet

Now I see a future
of broken bones
sneaky splinters and no
time for the Emergency Room

Observer

The Charge Nurse welcomes me into the OR
it's time you saw a c-section

borrowed scrubs don't cover my ass
my thin yellow gown sticks

the nurse inserts a line
the anesthesiologist inserts another
the patient's socks stop quivering

the surgeon draws a blue line
low and intentional
a scalpel and a laser open her
to yellow fat
thick and waxy
he moves the ropy muscles
her uterus bulges

a hairy head appears
the suction bulb too
a cry immediate, resounding
it's a girl, he says

the motion doesn't stop—
cut the cord
lift the baby—nurse to nurse—
heart monitor sings
placenta out
uterus intact

everything back together now—
her abdomen a strata of impossible stitches

I look at her body
the fleshy intimacy
paper drape between us

the blood suction tubing
bleeding washcloths tossed
the unforgiving striped linoleum

Grief

She knew he'd be still,
but wasn't prepared
for his soft skin—
    the tiny hands folded
    his sleep eternal
    the slack in his dimples.

I watched her sing
to him—*una canción de amor*
for what was lost.

The priest arrived, gave his
blessing, signed the cross on his
dusky forehead.

I didn't know
what else to say.

No, Thank You

A snarl of snot hangs
on the lip
of the sleeping baby.

Three-year-old fingers
touch thisandthatandovertheretoo
seeking tree frogs
for the kiddie pool.

The doe-eyed dog waits—
drooling and patient—
a goldfish cracker
(so close!)
in clumsy fingers.

I watch you wrestle
three sunscreened faces
two bottles of milk
a screeching toddler and a
bag of floaties.

My sister doesn't think
I understand, but
I know what I'm giving up.

Talking to Myself

These eggplant walls are so garish.
What would Gwendolyn Brooks think? Would lilac let you forget?
Can you hear the suction in the waiting room?
How long do we wait for Sarah W.?
Yes, sir, I will follow written orders.
I willingly sign my name to this legal chart.
My pen runs out mid-note.
Is Xanax contraindicated with Mifepristone?
I'll bet she's Catholic. What kind of cover story does she want?
Did I forget my lunch in the car? Everyone knows that you can't leave
anything out there—the protestors are outside.
I hate that the Xerox machine skips a page—always the fifth consent form.
Maybe I should be more scared about her bleeding.
Sounds like she'll survive. Sounds like she should leave her boyfriend.
Sounds like she should run.

Entering the Madhouse

The long hall waits for no one,
she says as she opens the door
to nowhere.

In the atrium,
a curled grasshopper is
paralyzed on the plant as a leathered
tail disappears into the coffee bark.

This coffee is burnt and stale
as the sad sacks explain their
comedies and tragedies—an untrustworthy
curtain of regrets and transgressions.
In the corner, Ophelia rolls her eyes.

I can't tell if I'm the grasshopper or
the lizard in this tragic Theater
of the Disinfected Linoleum.
What happens if I jump?
What happens if I disappear?

Family Zoom

I've been polite.
I've stifled my rage.
A Good Girl never talks back.

Even as a liquid screen
separates you from me,
I can't dodge your spitting
anger—mean and ugly—
as you roar your way
through your bullet points,
an echo chamber of ego.

You might think I'm smiling.
But I'm watching
your tongue slash
your logic into ribbons.
I'm waiting
to click off my camera.

Protest

It was May that we picketed—
the Washington Mall packed
with curious tourists
satin sashes
pop-up drummers
crimson knits

reminders of our continental continuity
our separate statehoods
one motherhood
one falsehood
one hooded cloak of the Grim—
catching fire in our teeth
as we marched our way down the block

How to Enter the Ring

We enter the fray
hand-in-hand—
one glove laced
with the same blood.

I split myself to please the crowd:
my repeating foe is me.

Lady versus Lady—
one life trapped in the crisp white dress
the other on display in permanent ink.

Toll the bell already.

I envision the roughhouse:
my future stains the satin,
red thorns bloom into
deep honesty.
How will we know who wins?

I spit on the lover
as I embrace the spar.
My inner women equally
wild and polite.
Kick her out of her comfort zone!
Smear blood on her teeth!
Make her earn those scars.

One cheekbone shatters,
another tooth gone for good.
Can you smell the sweat
as I taste the rush?

Maybe you should listen for the
thrust of the uppercut,
the swish of the almost-there.
My breast bruises from the ropes.

Ask me again to fight.

Wednesday

10:30 on a school night and
this married couple is stuck
on a sea theme puzzle,
rough coral and waving
anemones invite us
the siren song of suburbia

I look for the straight edges first—
how predictable a wife can be

Trying to order chaos
I skim the scorched rock,
ponder the secrets of this Atlantis—
are we building a city or exposing one?

I catch myself looking
for the striated and smooth,
the velvet boldness of red-on-red
I fit the pieces together and
fantasize about the crimson folds:
    a vintage movie theater curtain
    rumpled sheets, a red-light photo shoot
    a sultry saxophone in a sweating bar

I finger a cobalt patch—
how the neon longs for
    late-night clubs, house music
    short skirts, fuck-me pumps

the forest of cardboard
taunts my fingerprints
the stiff pulp electric with want

Hedera, or Scenes from a Marriage

If you stop to notice, you can see the creeping leaves
crawling on our doorframe, skulking around the windows.
You can almost hear the slow slither as the ivy sneaks
into our polite country house.

How does the limestone feel
to the sticky tentacles— does the vine
caress the stone or produce an unreachable
itch? Is it love or a fungus?

How can you stop the kinky green from twirling
into our lives? What more does it want?

Beware the mystery of aggressive simplicity,
reaching toward the rooftops
with only rock and time in its path.

Our House

At our house, they see me when they need me—
I am fur and bone, curious tail and wet nose,
I am the secret of their love.

In the mornings, she *plink-plinks* food into my plastic bowl,
opens the back door, scratches my triangle chin.
At our house, they hear me when he needs

an alarm clock—I leap heavily into their rumpled
blankets. His eyes smell like sleep.
I bring joy to the bedroom.

After I check for squirrels, I nose
my way into separate laps. I lick their open toes.
At our house, they see me.

After I've rolled in the hot grass,
I bring my plush to typing hands. I fill the house with fur.
I am love in the afternoon.

When we snuggle at night,
I take over the bed with clumsy paws.
At our house, they see me when they need me:
I stretch myself between them.

The Birthday Present

black yarn
pointed needles
a ninja appears

a red sash
over a plush belly
the stuffing disappears

an unthreatening aunt
builds gold throwing stars

for the hurricane toddler
a secret identity grows

maybe this will
teach him
how to be a man—

when to relish the soft
when to fight back

Janus

In the hallway, I steady my shoulders
study the white rose
enter with a soft voice

she rocks the lifeless blanket
catalogs tiny toes
elfin ears
I hear her pray
Mother Mary full of grace
into tiny feathers of hair

my pocket trills

the moment breaks
in *Español*

I sweep into the next room—
an ear-splitting caterwaul—
a baby boy, furious

the new father struggles
the mother clucks from the stiff bed
tok-tok-tok
between the shrieks, I coo—
a calm responder with an active bomb
pss-pss-pss-pss-pss
finally
the new diaper sticks

afterward,
I lay out the blanket—
quiero ayudar con las sabanas
let me show you how to swaddle

On Hearing Screams

Alone in the evening light,
we listen to the wind
howling howling
as if the Devil himself
was caught
finally
in my neighbor's raccoon trap,
an airy sprite seized
between chaos and purpose
between rage
and an eternity of spinning

the first thing to do
is find the source
the second thing
is to dash toward the yowl—
to charge your heart
into the uproar
to embrace the frantic
in the bones

Sex in a Red State

your hand
clutches
my breast
craves
your fingers
stroke
I want to
let go
but I can't shake
the ghost in the corner
your mouth
nibbling
my doubt
niggling
what if
you devour me
what if
the condom fails
I'll be trapped
your arms
tighten
what if we
keep going
my eyes
open
maybe we should
stop

Conviction

What can I say?
I've seen a protester come over to the clinic
when laws allow.
Have seen a corpse there.
Have held hands with a teenager wearily absorbing the ultrasound.
Was head over heart.
Have seen beyond hard trimesters.
I catalog medications, read badly written scripts.
Every story is shaded with stress.
Have seen that women are ants under glass.
Can't shield them all from the sun.

I badly want to shout.
Always polite.
I say I live with rebellion.
Can't reconcile Norma from Jane.
What danger is next, only the fiercest passion pulling me along
dizzyingly.
Nevertheless
we trust women—fighting, angry, flashing.

The Supreme Court flickers on the news.
The mad senators wait with their grubby hands
even as
even as women speak their tired truths.
And the protestors pounce,
often grabbing their children.
Listening less to reason over yelling.
They demand.
After shrill shouting (the woman within cringing) their pious throats
into a cavern—
sad boisterous nothings.
Little vampires in bloody tracksuits.

We know what it feels like to suck
a deep energy from marrow, eagerly even—
crying from losing. He with the scalpel scraping carefully
with his hands and voice, my supporting
is the strength without force, your clenched fist
near the vacuum, greedily sucking like a breast pump.

An Anti-Ode to the Call Light

you are a magical
red button. once pressed,
you flash to life,
trilling a regular jig of
hopeful need
DING
-dong-DING
-dong
How can I help you?

at the nurse's station
I have no idea what
your need could be—
accident, choking baby,
hemorrhage, fainting lady,
glass of water
How can I help you?

a few thousand false cries
for help and your magic
is gone. your siren haunts me—
an unceasing serenade
How can I help you?

away from the hospital,
I hear you in my sleep—
your golden hope the music
of my nightmares. always
alarmed, I race
to you in dreams
How can I help you?

Like it or not,
I can't ignore
your metallic cry—the
motherless newborn,
insatiable and urgent

How can I help you?
over and over and over

Drowning

On the day before
Mother's Day, you arrived
on a stretcher.
Your medical history—
cocaine
marijuana meth
domestic violence
homelessness
three suicide attempts
CPS

I carried your
daughter in my arms,
unable to rock her
back to life.

You hiccupped.
I watched your flannelled
boyfriend seethe, whisper-
ed threats growing louder,
drowning out your sobs.

I treated your pain. I
held your hands. I
sat with your moans. I
couldn't save her. I
can't save you.

after the Instagram photos

16 steps
never looked more
distant

you stand
up and
bleed
I hold
steady

there are six tubes
between you and the porcelain

I am safe
I am strong
I am here

we step together
a macabre slow-dance
your naked feet cautious
my ugly shoes sturdy
you cry the whole way there

I lower you to the seat
change your bloody pad
help you wash your labia
you are strong enough to walk back

we stand
careful not to pinch your tubes
we shuffle back to bed

only 3 steps away
and you
stop
panicked
your hands flutter in need
they hear your gag in the hall
a blue bag now warm with vomit

I am strong enough to hold
you in a partial hug
to reassure you
this is normal

you stop
breathe
sit

I reconnect you to the machines
clean off teary cheeks

you are safe
you are strong
you are here

16 steps and I'm the sweating one

helping you is
work

Remote Work

Tonight, I hear you move in the kitchen—
the sturdy pop of a French white,
the whisper flick of vanilla wax,
the *crash-bang-clang* of the dishwasher.

From the giant desk,
I watch you in the light
of our overpriced chandelier,
checking the score,
ordering groceries—

so many things I should say to you
in the deep midnight of who we've become.

In Case We Forget

In the ancient city,
the street performers
dance. Children sing
of jasmine and ivy.

Here, the plaza bends
around curious
tourists. Knick-knacks
are on sale.

Locals heave-ho
white tea leaves,
celebrate cicadas.

We did not prepare for the heat.

How, love, did we find ourselves
in sultry air, this yawning afternoon?
Our clothes cling to sweating skin,
aching to be tossed.

Let's inhale the incense,
this tropical anywhere—
full of possibility—
decide who we could be.

On Keeping Secrets

Twenty years in, I find myself
giggling with you at a burger joint,

surprised how well you know me—
my core fear of cockroaches,

what I always say when I'm drunk,
which superhero I secretly root against.

I know you too—
what YouTube videos put you to sleep,

which comedians make you cackle,
what kind of underwear you prefer.

As we replay the hits,
K-Ci & JoJo enter the chat

and we sing ourselves
into the street—
all my life, I've prayed for someone like you

I won't tell anyone it's your favorite.

Fig Tree

When we saw the listing, I fell in love,
gathered Granny's recipes,
waited to hand-press the jam.

What we got was a stonefruit tree,
unproductive, its fencepost
partially eaten by the dog.

Season over season,
the fig leaves cycle
in and out of vivid and brittle.

On the leafless days, I count
the bare branches, wait
for the roots to die.

On the sun-fluffed days, I suspect
the lush green canopy is the mirror
I avoid: fruitless and vulnerable.

My Friend Tells Me
for L.S.

I think I am losing my mind.
Everything around me is
sticky sticky sticky.
I can't remember why we did this.

Everything around me was
moving on fast-forward.
I can't remember why. We did this—
we made this formal decision.

Fast moving and forward,
I think about how
we made this formal decision.
He entered the world pink and screaming.

I think about how
my decisions now are bite-sized.
He enters the room pink and screaming.
I feel like screaming.

Biting into the size of my decisions,
I have an ongoing argument with a toddler.
I feel like screaming,
but this was our choice.

My toddler is winning the ongoing argument.
I am afraid that this will be my life forever.
Was this my choice?
I think I'm losing my mind.

Souvenirs (or, Things Happy Hour Cannot Solve)

1
Today, I unpack
sand-specked bikini bottoms;
two pairs of broken flip-flops;
pony beads—fat and hopeful—
from my niece's overpriced beach braids;
exploded glitter sunscreen in my checked luggage,
the sparkles we wore when we were mermaids.

2
I scroll and find the blurry selfie of her
asleep on my lap at the seafood restaurant.
I think about her even breathing,
her glasses askew, her four-year-old body curling
into my elbow, her breath on my knee.

3
That cheesy shot glass from the beach resort
mocks me from the liquor cabinet—
as if I could drown my longing in a Sex on the Beach,
as if we could have had Apple Jacks for breakfast,
as if a Purple Haze would make me rethink my plans,
go back in time, pray harder for a daughter.

Date Night

we arrive early
wait to be seated

on the east wall, a
mural begs for attention:

an open pot awaits the salmon
onions march to the chopping block
frogs creep out of the lake
an alligator lurks

on the left, a greedy mustache sharpens
the butcher knife, ready to cook

behind us, we hear
the small kitchen bustle
the plates clang
the galley radio low

...

if we had had a daughter,
by now she would have been 22

...

the savory broth
compliments the rye

we ignore the art
make small talk
try not to slurp

how polite we've become
how bland

Don't Leave Me

Someday, I will be
a mound of ashes.
With any luck, you'll spread me
somewhere lush—
the rain will soak me
into the ground, the wind will carry me
to the cranny whispers of the forest.

Or maybe,
you'll decide to plant me
under green-gold hydrangeas—
I'll bloom for you every summer,
a reminder of how much care
a wife needs
in the shade.

Perhaps you'll sprinkle me
over the ocean, just outside Bora Bora—
I'll become a pearl,
a haunting around someone else's neck.

Whatever you do,
don't leave me
in a mason jar, bouncing
around the trunk of your filthy car.
You should have listened to me,
to where I wanted to go.

If all else fails, bury me
in the backyard, across
from the lizard oak tree,
next to our favorite dog—
the one who loved me most.

Ode to my Size Elevens

I put so much pressure on you: the fleshy
ball, the broken fourth. The high arch waits
for a hand-knit sock. Were cowboy boots
a bad idea? The ankle tattoo was an homage.
We're in this together—

Walk. Run. Stand.
Bend. Plant. Curl.
Balance.

Remember Las Vegas? Thirty Bandaids
in 12 hours, those silly heels. I should tickle
you more. We can't run
from genetics. The second longer
than the first becomes the pained twist

in my grandmother's bare feet, a bunion
with a permanent screw. I never thank
you properly for the ability to sprint,
the survival of a long day,
the silent blister oozing,
the pressure

of hospital-friendly shoes.

Aggregate Data

I have seen a number of strange things in the hospital.
Ex: three years, fourteen stillbirths, fifty-six units of blood.
Sometimes these things are too unusual to count.

I've been a marriage counselor for a terrified couple,
a bouncer for an abusive spouse, a rock after an infant removal.
I have been a number of strange things in the hospital.

I have taught a new father how to swaddle a screamer,
a new mother to feed the insatiable, a new grandmother to hold her tongue.
Sometimes these things are too (extra)ordinary to count.

I've treated preeclampsia, hemorrhage, joy, sorrow, rage;
wrapped a dying infant, refereed a fight, sung *Row, Row, Row Your Boat.*
I have done a number of strange things in the hospital.

He trabajado in español, in Creole, in Arabic, and Somali;
I have learned the common language of blood and childbirth.
Sometimes there is nothing more to say.

Every day, I track the minor details of other people's lives:
She ate breakfast, she walked slowly, she mourned the adoption.
I've seen a number of strange things in the hospital.
Sometimes these things are too innumerable to count.

Things We Cannot Say

across town, the hospital is always awake
we line our pockets with gauze
we step into the inexhaustible
room after room after room

one is a first-timer
    one has a birth plan
        one has six mouths at home
one lives three hours away
    one second-guesses the adoption
        one is rocking the still

we can't prepare them
for strangers poking at a swollen belly swollen ankles prematurity
preeclampsia pain pain pain ear-splitting screaming hemorrhage uterine
massage intractable vomiting bleeding nipples crying overpriced supplies
inflated hospital bills nosy in-laws postpartum depression postpartum
anxiety weight retention post- post- post- months of no sex lifetime
stretchmarks failing bladders no maternity leave no more pain meds no
time to rest

all we can do is follow the state script
HIPAA's secrets burning
our throats, the mad
desire to say the right thing
the thing that won't haunt them
during a 3am feeding

the newborn sucking
the life out of them

Second Honeymoon

When you meet
me under the wild
howler moon, I will kiss

your hands with joy,
my fingers threading
the shadows of open

palm trees, a ruby
boat rocking against
vanilla sand.

Heat Lightning

September shouldn't feel this hot
but here we are—
the back porch on broil

humid, intimate
out in the open
the longing in my solar plexus

pinpricks of sweat trickle
as we sit and watch the flashes—
hot and jagged—cross the sky
how dangerous your hand

on my neck where your greedy mouth insists
you kiss my right-there-go-back
to beg for your tongue, to be devoured
electrified by want

grazing my knee

you inch my hem up my thigh

Punica granatum, or Directions to the Underworld

I open the red
tug on the white
discover a labyrinth.

I pluck a pygmy planet—
the magenta squish
sours my skin—
what indelible ink.

A plump kernel slips
through practiced fingers,
my fertility offering to the gods.

Careful now,
I pick off the berries from the
thin white honeycomb,
pulling at the curtain between here

and the hereafter, the divide
crumbling in my hands.

Notes

The epigraph to begin this collection is politely borrowed from Marge Piercy's poem "The Sabbath of Mutual Respect" from her 1980 collection *The Moon is Always Female* (published by Alfred A. Knopf, Inc, New York). While I have loved this poem (and Marge Piercy) for years, I chose this section of her work specifically to ground potential readers in this moment of history.

On September 1, 2021, *Senate Bill 8 (the Texas Heartbeat Act)* went into effect in the State of Texas. This bill prohibits a physician from performing or inducing an abortion after a fetal heartbeat has been detected (ie: abortion is illegal after ~6 weeks gestation). More has been added since— it is now a first- to second-degree felony for a physician to perform the abortion; there are vaguely-worded exceptions about risk of death or serious bodily impairment to the pregnant woman; and there are civil rewards for bounty-hunters who sue anyone who monetarily, logistically, or medically supports a woman in obtaining an abortion.

On June 24, 2022, the U.S. Supreme Court ruled on *Dobbs vs. Jackson Women's Health Organization*, which challenged a Mississippi ban on abortion at 15 weeks of pregnancy. This ruling effectively ended the federal constitutional right to abortion in the United States (which had been protected by *Roe vs. Wade, 1973*), sending the question back to each individual state to make decisions about how reproductive healthcare should be legislated.

As a result of these recent events, it is extremely challenging for women in conservative states to obtain abortion services.

I have dedicated my personal and professional life to supporting the health care needs and rights of women. *Pulling At the Curtain* is written from my own perspective as a woman serving and supporting the needs of other women, with an acknowledgment that I can only speak for myself. While I ground this collection in my own experiences, I recognize that countless unsung women have screamed, fought, lived, and died for my right to make my own reproductive choices.

This book is for them, for you, and for the courage we must all have to reclaim our bodies, our stories, and our reproductive rights.

Acknowledgements

Thank you to the editors of these journals in which these pieces have previously appeared, sometimes in slightly different form:

Beginnings: "Grief, "Ode to My Size Elevens," and "Try to Keep Up"

medmic: "Family Planning," "Aggregate Data", and "Conviction" https://medmic.com/three-poems-by-mary-jane-philpy-dollins/.

The Poetry Machine:

    Vol. 2 : "Entering the Madhouse," "Middle Age," "Family Zoom"

    Vol. 3: "The Point"

I am grateful for all of the poetry teachers and workshops that have helped to shape the pieces in this collection. This is not an exhaustive list, but I am very thankful for Elizabeth Ayres and Stacia Fleegal from the Center for Creative Writing; one-to-one editing time with Ellen Collins and Teneice Durrant; Sarah Ann Winn at the Writer's Center; KB Brookins through the Austin Public Library; and to the Loft Literary Center.

At the time of this writing, I am the President of the Austin Poetry Society. Garrison Martt has been incredibly helpful and I am grateful to all the APS members who have supported the evolution of this book.

Annie Przypyszny has spent many hours and sessions talking me through poetry versions, verb tenses and adverbs, even as she is progressing through an MFA program. She has been a rock star micro-editor.

Laura Van Prooyen has guided this book through several meaningful iterations and I cannot begin to thank her for the time, effort, and oversight necessary to bring this collection into being. I will sing her praises loudly for anyone who asks!

I'm also grateful for Amber Morena and her excellent help with layout and book design. I've never been so pleased to answer questions about font and line breaks.

Additional thanks to the family and friends who have listened to poetry drafts, who have used my pieces as a springboard into good conversation, and who have been tireless cheerleaders for the publication of this book. Thank you for all you've done to bring this book to life.

There are no words for the amount of patience, listening, and support that I have received from my husband Clay Dollins. I am grateful for you every day, but especially in this area of my life. Thank you for your encouragement, love, and all the M&Ms that helped with the writing process.

Mary Jane Philpy-Dollins
September 2024

www.ingramcontent.com/pod-product-compliance
Lightning Source LLC
Chambersburg PA
CBHW020806130626
46554CB00006B/2315